Y0-DOI-438

Family
RELATIONSHIPS

Chuck Smith

Maranatha Evangelical Association
Costa Mesa, California 92626 U.S.A.

© 1977 by Maranatha Evangelical Association.
All rights reserved. No part of this book may be
reproduced in any form without written permission
from Maranatha Evangelical Association.

Scriptural quotations based on the King James Version of
the Bible unless otherwise specified.

Library of Congress Cataloging in Publication Data

Smith, Chuck
  Family relationships.

  1. Family—Religious life.   I. Title.
BV4526.2.S53   248'.4   76-44496

ISBN 0-89337-005-3

PRINTED IN THE UNITED STATES OF AMERICA

Maranatha Evangelical Association
P.O. Box 1498
Costa Mesa, CA 92626

CONTENTS

Introduction

A man's life exists on two planes—a horizontal and a vertical. On the horizontal plane we relate to one another. On the vertical plane we relate to God. These two planes are on a fixed, centered axis.

Often we find that our horizontal plane is out of kilter, and we seek to correct this plane. We find ourselves unbalanced—so we try to rearrange or adjust our interpersonal relationships in order to reach an equilibrium. We're always trying to get our lives in balance, for we desire a well-balanced life. The difficulty seems to lie in the fact that as soon as we get one problem solved, two more arise. It seems impossible to maintain right relationships with everyone.

For instance, things may be going great at the job, but the situation at home is miserable. So we work on the home situation and get things smoothed out there, but then everything starts falling apart on the job. We find ourselves constantly struggling to reach and maintain this horizontal balance.

In reality, the answer to a well-balanced life doesn't lie in correcting the horizontal plane. The answer lies in correcting the vertical plane of our lives. A right relationship with God will affect every other relationship we have and, thus, bring the horizontal plane into balance. Jesus said, "Seek ye first the kingdom of God, and his righteousness; and all these things will be added unto you" (Matt. 6:33).

The weakness of psychology is that psychologists, seeking to help you with your interpersonal problems, often deal only with symptoms. But the heart of the problem lies in your relationship with God, and, until this is right, nothing else can be right.

By turning to the Word of God, we find how to have a right relationship with God—through a wholehearted belief in Jesus Christ as Saviour. We also find how to have a right relationship with one another—obedience to God's ordained principles. The Word then leads us to the specific principles ordained by God for love and harmony in the family.

This brief study of Colossians 3 and Ephesians 6 focuses on the important principles for strengthening family relationships, with suggestions for practical application. May this book encourage you in the further study of God's Word where the commands of God and the promises of His many blessings are found.

The True Test

The true test of Christianity isn't in the church but in the home. It isn't how saintly or godly you can act in the church, it's how your Christianity works in practical, everyday, living situations.

If I can't live the Christian life in the home, then I'm only a phony when I live it outside. It isn't difficult to look and act like a Christian when we come to church. We come, we sing, we worship the Lord, and we get "in the Spirit." I'm not saying that we're insincere—but it has to be demonstrated in the home, too.

I need to live the Christian life around those closest to me, those whom I rub shoulders with daily. My relationship with Christ should definitely affect my relationship with my wife. And because of my relationship with Christ, I should have a better relationship with my wife.

Dr. Parker, the famous minister, was speaking to a church in Chicago. After a few nights of services in which the Lord had been blessing through the study of the Word, there was a sharing time. People told of the blessings they were receiving through Dr. Parker's ministry and the Word of God. One lady stood up and said, "I'm so thankful for these lessons and what they've done for me! I'm so thankful that God loves me! I'm so thankful for this relationship that I have to God in Jesus Christ!"

She started to sit down. Dr. Parker said, "Just a moment. Tell me, with this new relationship in Jesus Christ, how does that affect you in the home? Does this make you a better mother? Does it make you a better housewife? Are you now performing the duties of the home without murmuring and complaining? Are you sweeter to your husband because of your relationship wth Christ? Has this really made you a better wife and housekeeper? . . ."

He felt a tug on his coat and the minister behind him said, "Press those points, brother! That's my wife!"

Our Christian experience should find its expression within our home relationship. But, we must confess at the outset, the application of Christian principles isn't easy. We can attest to the truth and acknowledge what is right, but the difficulty arises in putting it into practice.

The blending of two lives into one is never a smooth operation. There are always those difficulties that do arise. Thus, we find the market flooded with books on marriage. People are buying these books and pouring through them in the hope of discovering some new secret or new formula for a happy and peaceful arrangement within their homes.

The situation is similar to the perennial problem of weight control. Everyone is coming up with a new scheme promising *the* answer. "Without dieting or exercising you can lose 50 pounds! Very simple! Just mail $10 for these exciting secrets." We're always looking for that easy road to happiness and success.

In reality, there is no easy road. A successful, happy relationship takes a lot of work. The blending of two lives into one is a difficult experience.

Paul was very wise in couching his remarks by saying, "Above all these things put on love, which is the bond of perfectness" (Colossians 3:14). It is only through the love of God working in and through our lives—and our yielding to that love of God working in and through our lives—that we can ever come to a successful, happy blending of our two lives into one.

The Real and the Ideal

Each of us has his own idealization of himself. There's the "real" you and there's the "ideal" you—the ego and the superego. Supposedly, the degree of divergence between the ego and the superego is a criterion of a person's mental well-being. If there's a vast distance between the real you and the ideal you, you're a troubled person—a neurotic. If the difference between the real you and the ideal you is slight, then you're supposedly a well-adjusted person.

But who is the "real" you? It seems everybody knows that but you—because you've built-up an idealization of yourself. There's the saying, "A happy wife is the greatest compliment to her husband"—because somehow he believes he's the reason for her happiness. The "ideal" me is the way I see myself. The "real" me is the way others see me. Quite often these viewpoints are far apart. It's hard for me to know the real truth about myself and, as a result, I'm unwilling or reluctant to accept responsibility or blame for any problems that may exist within the home.

"It really isn't my fault!" As Adam said, "Lord, the woman that *thou* gavest to be with me" (Genesis 3:12). We're always seeking to pass our failures on to someone else. It could never be *my* fault. *I* could never really be to blame. "If *he* would only straighten up!" "If *she* would only do what the Scripture tells her to do, then our marriage could be happy and successful!" We're always looking for the changes to come upon the other person's part and not upon our own. I'm convinced that in every situation there needs to be changes on **both** parts.

Understanding the Differences

The Bible says, "Male and female created he them" (Gen. 1:27). It doesn't take a genius mentality to realize there's a difference between male and female. This we all recognize. But there are differences we fail to recognize between the sexes that are important—differences that need to be recognized if we're to have a happy blending of the two.

When God first created man, God recognized that man by himself was not complete. Man by himself can never be complete. God said, "It is not good that the man should be alone" (Gen. 2:18). God created the woman so that through her the man might find and have completeness, companionship, love—that which he could not get from all the animal kingdom. For Adam dwelt among the animal kingdom and God didn't find among them any help that was suitable for him. God created the woman in order that she might be that completeness for man.

In creating woman God created her different from man in physical structure—the man being the stronger and larger, the woman being the smaller and more frail.

Along with the physical differences, certain emotional differences were created. In the emotional realm He created the woman with a higher sensitivity than the man. Emotionally, man is usually very coarse. His emotions move in a narrower spectrum. A woman's emotional spectrum is quite wide. She's capable of great highs; she's capable of great lows. Yes, a man can get excited and a man can get depressed. But, as a general rule, he cannot appreciate as much as a woman or enjoy as much as a woman. Men don't have the extreme highs that women can attain.

As far as intelligence is concerned, I don't believe that there's any difference at all between male or female. I believe that women are capable of as great an understanding and thinking process as men. Spiritually, of course, men and women are one in the eyes of God (Galatians 3:28).

But, having created us with different physical characteristics and a different emotional spectrum, God then set forth the rules of the relationship between husband and wife. By obeying these rules, man and woman could find the fulfillment, joy, and happiness from life that God desires them to have.

God's Rules of Order

I believe that God loves you and has a wonderful plan for your life. I'm convinced of that. I believe that God wants your life to be **filled** with joy. I believe that God wants your life to be as an overflowing cup. I believe that God wants the best for you as His child, even as a parent wants the best for his child. I believe God is a very wise and loving Father who is concerned with the joy and happiness of His children. He is grieved when you're unhappy, despondent, or having problems. I believe God's desire for you is a full, rich, abundant life. Jesus said, "I am come that they might have life, and that they might have it more abundantly" (John 10:10).

Thus, God set forth certain principles or rules in His wisdom, knowing how He had created us, knowing our capacities and capabilities, and knowing our needs. He set up His rules and said, "This is the way to joy, happiness, peace, love, and a rich life."

Our problem is that we don't always agree in practice with what God has said. We may agree in principle. But we soon get to that place of divergence between the principle and the application. So, if you ask me whether I believe the Bible—yes. Do I always practice what the Bible espouses—no. And whenever I violate one of the rules, I'm the one who suffers.

God's rules are really the rules of happiness. They are the rules of success. David said, "Blessed [how happy] is the man . . . [whose] delight is in the law of the Lord; and in his law does he meditate day and night. And he shall be like a tree planted by the rivers of water, that bringeth forth his fruit in his season; his leaf also shall not wither; and whatsoever he doeth shall prosper" (Psalms 1:1-3). Moses told Joshua to take the law of the Lord and meditate in it day and night, "for then thou shalt make thy way prosperous, and then thou shalt have good success" (Joshua 1:8).

As I look at the rules God has set forth, I may say, "I could never be happy doing that." I may argue in my heart with the rules of God. But, in reality, I'll never be happy until I obey them. The world is filled today with frustrated people. They have that sense of life-is-passing-me-by. "There must be more to life than this!" Thus, there's that quest and search for fulfillment, for satisfaction, for something to take care of this crazy yearning within.

This is a result, really, from arguing with the rules that God has set up, and by trying to find happiness and peace apart from obedience to the command of God. God has set up a certain

14

order. You may argue with it, you may debate it, you may violate it. But you'll never find real peace, happiness, and joy until you submit to it.

The Christian Ethic

The first point that we notice about the Christian ethic is that it declares a reciprocal obligation. Under the ethics of the Greek philosophies, the Roman culture, and even the Jewish culture, there was no reciprocal obligation. The husband was the absolute master and the wife was a chattel. She had no rights.

The Christian ethic not only tells the wife's obligation to the husband, but the husband's obligation to the wife. Under the other ethics there was no obligation of the husband to the wife. The Christian ethic not only lists the child's obligation to the parent, but it lists the parent's obligation to the child. The Christian ethic not only defines the servant's relationship to the master, but the master's relationship and obligation to the servant.

We need to realize that the cause and effect consequence of spiritual laws is as certain as that of physical laws. If you violate the physical law of gravity by jumping off a high roof, you're going to suffer. Likewise, if you violate the spiritual laws that govern your relationships, you're bound to suffer. The Greeks used to say, "The dice of the gods are loaded." By this they meant that you couldn't win against God. His Word is sure.

Submission and Love

Women should be extremely thankful for Jesus Christ and Christianity, for, before the advent of Christianity, the woman's lot was barely above that of a slave's.

When we were in Guatemala we ran out of gas on the way to Antigua. The friends that were with us hiked ahead to buy some gas. As we were looking around and praising the Lord for the glorious beauties of this country, I heard the cracking of bushes up in the hills of this thickly forested area. I looked up and saw three women walking down from the mountains. I couldn't even see a trail. They were carrying huge bundles of sticks, probably weighing 50 to 75 pounds each, on their heads. They'd been out in the forest chopping wood all day long. They were now carrying these bundles home so they could cook the food.

In Israel we saw many of the Bedouins. The women were out in the field. They were plowing, they were pulling the weeds, they were planting; meanwhile their husbands were sitting around, trading sheep and drinking coffee.

These women in Guatemala and Israel labor. They have very few rights or privileges. Christianity has done much for women.

In his epistle to the Colossians, Paul starts with the women. "Wives, submit yourselves unto your own husbands, as it is fit in the Lord" (Col. 3:18). Now, I've heard so much about submission that I'm sick of it. Many times by talking enough about something we can relieve ourselves of the obligation to do a certain thing. We can talk very glibly and skillfully about a woman's submission to her husband. The wives can get together and share how "we ought to be submitted." But by *talking* about it they can free themselves from the actual obligation of doing it.

There is one place in the Scripture where the wife led the husband. That was back in the Garden of Eden, and we've been in trouble ever since.

God's rule is that the husband be the head of the house and the wife submit unto the husband.

Naturally, there is an order involved. In this true order the husband is to be submitted unto Christ, even as Christ willingly submitted Himself unto the Father. As a husband is submitted to Christ and the wife is submitted to the husband, the wife in reality is submitted to Christ through the husband.

Ungodly Demands

I do not believe that the Scripture requires a wife to submit to ungodly demands of a husband. It is sheer stupidity to say that no matter what the husband says, you're to submit to it because you're the wife. Some teach this concept, saying that the Lord will keep you safe from any dire consequence if you submit. I do not agree with that.

Paul said, "Wives, submit yourselves unto your own husbands, as unto the Lord" (Ephesians 5:22). In 1 Corinthians Paul lays out the whole chain of command. The husband is, actually, the authority over the wife, Christ is the head over the husband, and God is the authority over Christ (1 Cor. 11:3).

If this chain of command is broken anywhere along the line, God's order is gone. The husband is the head over the wife only as Christ is the head over the husband. If Christ is not the head over the husband, then the wife should be in submission to Christ first. She skips over the broken link. Peter said to the Sanhedrin, "We ought to obey God rather than men" (Acts 5:29). That applies to the relationship in the home if the husband is making ungodly demands upon his wife.

First of all, a woman should be more careful concerning the man whom she marries. Determine whether or not he is the kind of person to whom you could submit *before* you marry him. If you doubt his judgment and think that he's so dumb now, why did you marry him in the first place? Maybe the Jewish culture was correct in arranging marriages. The Jews said that a decision as important as marriage should never be left to the capricious emotions of a teen-ager. I must admit that many marriages ought not to be. Yet, in the divine order of things, God's rule is "Wives, submit unto your own husbands."

If you have a godly husband, one who loves the Lord and is seeking the Lord, how glorious that is! How much easier that makes your position of submitting unto him. I read of a husband who was in a bar one night with some buddies. As the bar closed up he made a wager with them. He bet that, if they all went to his house, he could order his wife to wake up and fix them a dinner—and she'd do it without grumbling or griping but smiling the whole time. The guys took him up on his bet.

So, they staggered into his house past 2 a.m. He went in and told his wife to get out of bed and fix them a meal. She came out with a smile, went to the kitchen without any complaining, and prepared the food. Then she placed it on the table, smiling very cheerfully the whole while.

His buddies couldn't believe it. As they paid off their bet, they complimented her. "We had a bet with your husband that you wouldn't make a dinner. We lost, but this is worth seeing! How can you be so pleasant under such adverse circumstances?"

She said, "I'm a Christian. I love the Lord. I know that my stay here isn't going to be very long, and I'm looking forward to being with my Lord and the joys of dwelling with Him in heaven.

"My husband isn't a Christian. His future is so black that I thought I'd make it as happy as I could while he's still here." The husband became so convicted that within a week he accepted the Lord.

Drawing Closer Together

It is said that marriage is a 50-50 proposition. I hardly believe that. I believe marriage is a 100-100 proposition. If you only give 50 percent to it, you'll never make it. Both sides have to give 100 percent in order to have a really happy, successful marriage. I do believe that God's divine order is that the husband be the head of the house and the wife submit to the husband as is fit in the Lord.

As I said, the Christian ethic introduced the reciprocal obligation. Under the Christian ethic it declares, "Husbands, love your wives, and be not bitter against them [harsh with them]" (Col. 3:19). In the Greek or Roman ethic a husband didn't need to love his wife. In fact, according to the Greek philosophers, every man was supposed to have a mistress or concubine for his pleasure and a wife to bear his legitimate children.

But the Christian ethic says, "Husbands, love your wives." This word for "love" is the word *agape*, which is that giving, self-sacrificing love.

Agape is that love that God has for us when He so loved the world that He **gave** (John 3:16). This is the kind of love that a husband is to have for his wife. In Ephesians Paul made it a little stronger: "Husbands, love your wives, even as Christ also loved the church, and gave himself for it" (Eph. 5:25).

Now, we sometimes get off on the wrong foot in our relationships. We actually begin to work against one another. Many times, rather than submitting to her husband, a wife is rebellious—arguing against every decision he makes, rebelling against his authority, and challenging his wisdom and judgment. This, in a sense, destroys the husband's male ego. Thus, he responds and reacts to this by becoming cold and aloof.

The more aloof the husband becomes, the more the wife rebels against his authority. The more she rebels against his authority, the more aloof he becomes. Soon, every situation is pushing them further and further apart. Any decision he makes is challenged or rejected by her. Every decision brings on this big explosion, this big argument, this big division. Because of this, the man has a reluctance and unwillingness to demonstrate a love for his wife. Very possibly, at this point he may not even have a love for his wife. He has that coldness and aloofness.

The wife feels no security whatsoever, for security comes with love. Because she lacks a sense of security, she thinks, "How can I submit to him? I don't even know if he's concerned about me. He's just thinking of himself."

Now, if you can reverse the process, it draws the man and wife closer and closer together. The more a husband shows and demonstrates his love to his wife, the more secure she feels and becomes. The more secure she becomes in his love, the more readily she can submit unto his authority and his decisions. The more she submits, the more he loves her. So, you can get the process working in the right direction.

Unfortunately, in too many marriages the process is driving *apart* rather than drawing *together*. But which comes first, the chicken or the egg? Who gives in first? Does *he* demonstrate love first? Does *she* submit first?

Usually, a husband will say: "I tried. I demonstrated love. But she thought, 'I've got you! I'm going to insist on my own way now!'" The husband is afraid the wife will take advantage of the situation. On the other hand, the wife will say, "I submitted to him and he did the dumbest thing! So stupid!"

Where's it going to break? It's going to break in a divorce court someplace. You can actually keep driving yourself further and further from your mate by not being willing to yield.

Ideally, the problem should be faced with both of you on your knees confessing before the Lord your failure to obey and follow His law—the wife confessing her failure of obedience in submitting to her husband as is fit in the Lord, and the husband confessing both his failure to love his wife as Christ loved the Church and his bitterness or his harshness towards her. Then the husband and wife must seek through the help of the Holy Spirit to follow the scriptural pattern.

"God, help me to show her that kind of love in which she can feel secure so that she can submit." "God, help me not to argue, not to speak up when I think he's doing something that's dumb and stupid, but to keep my mouth shut and to go along with it—knowing that, even if we lose everything, we've still got each other, this love and You. That's all we need, Lord. Help me to be in submission unto him and his authority."

The Power of Obedience

The next relationship on Paul's list is that of the child to the parents. "Children, obey your parents" (Col. 3:20). Under the law of God the children were demanded to honor their parents—to show respect and to be obedient unto their parents. Paul said, "Children, obey your parents in the Lord: for this is right. Honor thy father and thy mother; which is the first commandment with promise" (Eph. 6:1).

Many of the promises of God are conditional. This is the first commandment that has a promise added to it as a blessing. "Honor thy father and thy mother: that thy days may be long upon the land" (Exodus 20:12). If a child didn't honor his parents or didn't respect them, they could take him before the elders of the city and say, "I have a stubborn, rebellious child. He's a glutton and a wine-drinker." The child would then be stoned to death. His days would not be so long upon the earth!

The Child's Former Lot

At the time Paul was writing the epistle to the Ephesians, the Roman empire had very little regard for children. The father was the absolute authority within the home for as long as he lived. If you were 50 years old and your father was alive, you were still in subjection to him. The father had the absolute rights over his children, even to their life and death. He could put them to death if he so desired. He could sell them as slaves. He could do whatever he wished with his children.

A letter was found which was typical of this absolute control. A husband had gone to Alexandria to engage in commerce. He wrote very lovingly to his wife. He talked to her concerning the child that she was expecting, apologizing for the fact that he had been delayed in Alexandria and wouldn't be home for the birth. He wrote, "If it's a boy, keep it. If it's a girl, throw it out."

Many children were thrown out. Almost every evening in the Forum, Romans would abandon the children that they didn't want. In the morning others would come by and pick up these children and raise them to sell as slaves. People had very small regard for children. It was not uncommon to just throw an unwanted child away.

Prior to the Roman rule, in some of the earlier periods in the land of Canaan where God brought the children of Israel, sacrifice of babies was not at all uncommon. In many of the homes uncovered by archaeologists, jars with infants' skeletons have been found embedded in the structures. It was a sign of good fortune and a good omen to place your baby in a jar and make it part of the wall when building the house. Infant sacrifice was a common practice.

Christianity has done much for children. It has caused us to honor and respect life and it has taught us to love. You may think it natural and instinctive to love your children, but there are non-Christian cultures which display no love for a child. Children are considered a burden, an obligation, and a responsibility.

In the midst of this Roman concept, Paul writes, "Children, obey your parents in the Lord: for this is right" (Eph. 6:1). In 2 Timothy 3:1 Paul told us, "In the last days perilous times shall come." One of the signs of the perils of the last days is that children would be disobedient to parents (3:2). In his letter to the Romans Paul is telling us of the decayed, corrupt condition of the heathen world—a world that was given over by God to a reprobate mind, given up by God to uncleanness. As Paul lists the horrible con-

ditions of a depraved world, he writes of dis-
obedience to parents as a sign of moral decay
(Rom. 1:30).

In The Lord

The Scriptures say, "Children, obey your parents." Notice that there is a qualification. "Obey your parents **in the Lord:** for this is right" (Eph. 6:1). It does follow that there are some parents who are not honorable. It would be impossible to honor them for the kind of life that they live. There are some demands made by parents which would violate a person's Christian conscience to obey. A child is not obligated to obey an ungodly demand of a parent. There are some parents—undeserving of the title of father or mother—who would lead their children into all kinds of ungodly practices.

I've had counseling with many unfortunate cases of teen-age girls being assaulted or molested at an early age by their fathers. To me that is the most horrible, sickening thing a man could do. I don't think a beast would do something that low. Thus, I do not think a child must, because he is a child, submit to that kind of lust or insanity.

What happens in cases where moral issues are not involved? For instance, "I want to go to church tonight and my parents said, 'No, you'd better do your homework.' " In that case you'd better do your homework. There's no moral issue involved.

"Children, obey your parents in the Lord." How beautiful to have godly parents! At the top of the list of thanksgiving in my own life is my heritage of a godly mother and father. What a privilege, what a blessing, what a goodness of God to me that I had parents whom I could honor, respect, and obey. They loved God deeply and served the Lord with all their hearts and lives. A home filled with love—that's the kind of home God wants you to have for your children.

My heart goes out to many of the young people we deal with today. I'm not one to blame someone else for my faults. I believe in accepting the responsibility for the person that I am. The same rain falls on everybody and the same sun shines on everybody. There are those who go out in the rain and praise the Lord. There are others who say, "Curses! It's raining again!" There are those who say, "What a beautiful sunny day!" Others say, "It looks like it's going to be hot and miserable." Same rain, same sun. What do you do with it? What is your attitude towards it?

But I can understand, because of the environment in which they were raised, why many young people are what they are today. I don't use that as an excuse. You shouldn't say,

"My father has eaten sour grapes, so my teeth are set on edge." You can rise above your environment. You can rise above your circumstances. Thank God! That's the gospel of Jesus Christ.

Your father could be an alcoholic and your mother a prostitute. They could have deserted you from the time you were a one-year-old. You could have lived off the street—and still be a fantastic, powerful child of God. You can rise above any environmental background. You can't lie down and quit. "I've had such a horrible background! I've had such a horrible life at home! I can't be anything else but my mean, miserable, cantankerous self. I am what I am because of *them*!" You can't spend your whole life excusing your rotten, nasty attitude and disposition on your early childhood.

Through the power of the Holy Spirit you can rise above any type of environmental background that you may have experienced. We've seen it over and over again. When Jesus Christ deals with you, He can change you as an individual and make you a new creature. You don't have to relate back to your "Irish background." The new nature is now yours through Jesus Christ.

One of the beautiful witnesses that has happened here recently is the dramatic change in the lives of many young people accepting Jesus Christ. This has changed their attitude at home and with their parents. The parents, in turn, have become interested in what caused

Johnny to experience such a great change in his life. As a result, many parents have come to experience a new life in Christ. God has made and created many new Christian families as a consequence of the changed attitude of young people who have gone back home. Parents have been able to *see* the difference that Jesus Christ has made.

Fathers and Mothers

The Christian ethic isn't only "Children, obey your parents" but "Fathers, provoke not your children, lest they be discouraged" (Col. 3:21). It is tragic that many times we're guilty of discouraging our children.

I believe that a child can be discouraged by too much prohibition. We can put too many "no-no's" in his way.

When a child is growing up you should child-proof your home. If you have little knick-knacks that you don't want toyed with or broken, put them out of the child's reach rather than down within his reach. That way you don't have to say "No, no" every time he moves towards one of your prize possessions. There should be prohibition, but unnecessary prohibitions can discourage a child and give him a negative complex to begin his life with. I've seen little children walking around a room saying "No, no, no, no."

I believe a child can be discouraged by unfeeling and absolute government. We don't have to say "You do it because I said to do it!" Parents should be open and reasonable with children.

I think that a child can be discouraged by an overexacting, difficult-to-please manner. The other day at the beach a woman came out with her family and laid a blanket on the sand. She said, "Don't get any sand on the blanket! Watch out! Don't get sand in the food! Be careful! We're here to have fun, and we're going to have fun!" By then you're so wiped out that you're ready to go home. Nervous prattle is very discouraging to a child.

There's also the need to avoid constant displeasure with everything a child does. For example, when he shows you a picture that he colored and you say, "How come you went over the line here?"—that can be discouraging to a child. Children need encouragement. As parents we need to be careful. Many times we are too difficult in being pleased.

We can discourage a child in holding our displeasure too long. I think the moment a child repents and declares that he's sorry, we should drop the case at that point. Don't go on for days saying, "I can't believe you did it! Oh, I can't believe that!"—holding the guilt over him day after day. "My expensive china and it's broken!"

What if God did that to us? When we've done wrong and we ask God for forgiveness, we don't want Him to be long-faced and groaning for days over the fact that we blew it so badly.

I think that a child can be discouraged by

hasty and false accusations. I had a great dad, but he wasn't perfect. In fact, he was very excitable. And I had a younger brother, Bill, who was a real rascal. Before Bill was born, my father said to my mother, "If you'll have a redheaded boy, I'll buy you a Cadillac." I don't know how it happened, but she had a redheaded boy. My brother Bill was all boy, and my father really idolized him, as we all did. Bill came along later than the rest of us, and so we all babied him and spoiled him.

Whenever Bill would start screaming and crying, my father would almost go insane. And my brother Bill knew this. So, each time my other brother and I would ever do anything to displease Bill, he'd say, "I'm going to get you!"—and he'd start screaming. My dad would come running, pulling off his belt, and whip us older boys. *Then* dad would ask, "What's the matter in here?" Whenever brother Bill started screaming, we'd run—because my dad would belt first and ask questions later. I wasn't always innocent, but I was spanked many times when I wasn't even involved. That was part of my dad's excitable nature. He spanked first and asked questions later.

If we're constantly accusing our children falsely and being hasty in our judgment concerning them, that's very discouraging to them.

I believe a child is discouraged when he's constantly being suppressed because of possible danger. "No! You can't go out and play baseball. You might get hurt. You might hurt your finger. If the ball would hit your finger in the wrong way it would hurt and swell . . . You'd better not ride your bicycle. It's so dangerous to ride your bicycle." Well, living is dangerous. Constantly suppressing a child because of possible dangers can discourage him.

Now, as a parent you need to exercise prudence, judgment, and wisdom. I believe that children need to be warned of certain dangers, such as getting into cars with strangers. But there's no way you can watch them twenty-four hours a day and protect them from every hurt and injury. That's part of life and growing up.

I believe a child can be discouraged by giving him a test of character that is inappropriate for his age. For instance, if a little two-year-old should happen to lose his temper, you wouldn't say, "Oh! You've got a bad heart!" I heard of a little boy who had a chest x-ray. The doctor pointed out his heart on the x-ray and the little boy began to weep because it turned out that his heart was black. I think that holding a child in this heavy judgment for something that's not characteristic of his age discourages him.

I think that we discourage children by sometimes holding them aloof from the things of the Lord when they desire them. We say, "You're too young. You don't understand yet." Jesus said, "Whosoever shall not receive the kingdom of God as a little child, he shall not enter into it" (Mark 10:15).

For example, we might say to a 6 or 7 year-old who's sitting in a communion service and desires to take communion, "Oh no, you can't take that. You're too little." But in his heart he loves Jesus. Maybe he doesn't understand all the implications (I don't know whether I do), but I think children ought to be allowed to participate in spiritual things. As soon as they are old enough to understand what is happening—perhaps not with a full understanding, but even with that slightest understanding—they should be encouraged and allowed to participate in spiritual things.

"Fathers [the Greek reads "Fathers and mothers"], provoke not your children to wrath: but bring them up in the nurture and admonition of the Lord" (Eph. 6:4). One of the most tragic scenes that I have observed is a parent who needles or teases the child until he's driven to frustration and distraction. I've seen parents do it with small children—holding out a bottle, then pulling it away, laughing, holding it out, pulling it away. I see the little child teased until he doesn't know what to do. That's one of the cruelest things that a parent can do.

Instead, bring them up in the discipline and admonition of the Lord. Solomon said, "Train up a child in the way he should go: and when he is old, he will not depart from it" (Proverbs 22:6). It is our responsibility as parents to take time to teach, to train, and to bring up our children in the discipline and admonition of the Lord.

Discipline

By nature we are sinners. David said, "They go astray as soon as they be born, speaking lies" (Psalms 58:3). He recognized the perversity of his own human nature. There is a psychology or, more aptly, a philosophy of permissiveness. "Let them do what they want to do. Don't restrain them. Let them freely express themselves." I think that Dr. Spock in this philosophy has done a great disservice to our nation. A child left to his natural bent is not innately good but is innately evil and sinful. The Scriptures say that "foolishness is bound in the heart of a child; the rod of correction shall drive it far from him" (Prov. 22:15).

The word "discipline" (translated "nurture" in Ephesians 6:4) carries the connotation of discipline with punishment. It's a difficult task to train your children. It takes time. It's easier just to let them do things rather than to stop them. But the Scripture also says, "A child left to himself bringeth his mother to shame" (Prov. 29:15).

It is vitally important in the discipline of our

children that there always be a great conscious-
ness in their hearts of our love for them, that
they be secure in that love, and that, when they
are disciplined, they never doubt that love.

Every child is natural and when he's spanked
often says, "Nobody loves me anymore! You
hate me! You don't love me!" We hate to hear
such accusations from our children, and we
sometimes become slack or forebear punishment or discipline. In doing so we are harming
and hurting the child; for, when he knows that
he's done wrong, one of the best ways to be re-
lieved of that guilt complex is to be punished.
Many children are psychologically problemed
today. They are carrying around with them
guilt complexes which have never been re-
lieved by their permissive parents.

When I was a child and disobeyed my father,
he'd say, "All right, son. When you get home,
go into your bedroom. I'll come and talk with
you." I knew exactly what he meant. He did his
talking with a strap. But I knew that I had done
wrong. There'd be a wall between my dad and
me all the way home. I couldn't talk to him. I
was guilty. I was a culprit.

He'd come into the room and say, "Why did
you do it, son?"

"I don't know, Dad. I just did it."

"Son, I told you not to do it. But you did it
anyway. Why?"

"I don't know!" I really knew. I did it because I wanted to, but I didn't want to tell *him*
that.

"All right, son. I'll have to spank you for that." I'd get it. I'd yell. I found out that if I yelled I wouldn't get so many. I'd scream like I was dying. He'd leave the room feeling miserable, and I'd lie there for a while wishing I were dead. If I were dead then he'd be sorry for spanking me!

But after a while mother would call me for dinner. I'd bounce into the dining room. "Hi, Dad!" It was all right now. I wasn't guilty anymore! There was no wall between us now. I had been punished, therefore there was no more guilt. That was a past issue no longer hanging over my head.

There was nothing worse, though, than having done something wrong, yet not being caught for it. I would sit at the table but I couldn't look at my dad. He didn't know what I had done, but I was afraid that he might find out. The guilt could weigh so heavily on me that within two or three days I'd be completely miserable.

What a glorious relief when we finally face up to it and get it over with!

The Word

As parents we need to be careful never to punish our children in anger, because then we're prone to overpunish the child.

Many parents make a great mistake in threatening to punish their child. Never threaten to punish. Promise to punish him and never break your promise. Some parents threaten their children all the time. "I'm going to knock your head off if you do that again!" You're not going to knock his head off. You're constantly threatening until the child doesn't pay any attention to what you say. Just threats—and he knows it. But when your child learns that he can trust your word to be good, you won't have to yell at him anymore. All you have to do is speak.

Yelling is a sign of weakness. It's a sign of failure as a disciplinarian. I have to yell at my dog because I'm a failure at disciplining him properly. "Shut up, Sherman"—and he just keeps barking. But if I say, "SHUT UP, SHERMAN!" he gets quiet. Why? Because I'm lazy. I'm too lazy to get up and discipline him.

So many times the same is true of our children. We haven't learned to discipline them with a word. We've fallen into the bad habit of shouting. Paul wrote to Timothy, "From a child you've known the holy scriptures" (2 Tim. 3:15). Timothy had been trained, he'd been disciplined, he'd been brought up in the Word of God. What a blessing!

Children will not naturally gravitate towards good. You have to teach them the value of goodness, honesty, and moral integrity. You don't have to teach your child to cheat. They do that naturally. You have to teach them *not* to cheat. You never have to worry about teaching your child how to lie. They do that naturally. You have to teach them what is the truth and that they must always tell it. There's a natural bent towards the sinful nature. Children must be trained. They must be disciplined.

You must bring up children in the discipline and the admonition of the Lord. But when you do, you may go through some years of trial when, in that intermediate stage, they move from their parents' faith to the discovery of their own faith. You may go through some shaky years as they're getting out and trying their wings, but you always have the confidence that they'll return to the God of their early years and early training. So, don't panic. Know that the Lord is going to bring them back to Himself if you've been faithful in your training, and you'll be rewarded in their salvation.

Employer/Employee

Finally, the Bible speaks of "servants and masters" and defines certain rules for their relationship. Actually, we don't have bond slaves today. The whole scene has shifted from servants and masters to employees and employers. However, I think that we can apply the rules for "servant" to "employee" quite readily.

"Obey in all things your masters according to the flesh; not with eyeservice, as menpleasers; but in singleness of heart, fearing God" (Col. 3:22). I believe that you should be the most productive employee on your job as a witness for Jesus Christ. I believe that you should be honest and upright. You shouldn't spend much time visiting, even witnessing, on the job. You should give the job your fair share of labor and work.

You can and should witness during the breaks and lunch hours. But it's not a good witness to your employer if you're always witnessing to your co-worker when you should be working. Your employer is watching you and can see that you're keeping the fellow next to you from working. That's a bad witness for Christ. That's almost stealing from your employer. I feel that as an employee you should be extremely diligent. You should be a hard worker. You should seek to be the most profitable employee as a witness for Jesus Christ. Not with eyeservice, not as a man-pleaser, but doing it as unto the Lord. "Whatsoever ye do, do it heartily, as to the Lord, and not unto men; knowing that of the Lord you shall receive the reward of the inheritance [the true reward]" (Col. 3:23, 24).

"Masters, give unto your servants that which is just and equal; knowing that ye also have a Master in heaven" (Col. 4:1). The Bible has done a great deal for the laboring man. God is for the laboring man. God speaks out against unjust wages more than once. God says, "Go to now, ye rich men, weep and howl for your miseries that shall come upon you." The rich have actually defrauded and held back wages, and now their silver and gold are corrupted (James 5:1-4). God speaks against withholding a proper wage and salary. I believe the employer is obligated to give his employees a just and equal salary, but employees ought to earn it, too. "Knowing that ye also have a Master in heaven." You must always remember that there is one final Judge wherein we will all be judged. That is in God.

Summary

We have briefly looked at the human relationships that pertain to the particular role that I have in life—as an employer, as a father, as a husband, as a wife, as a mother, as a child, or as an employee. What is my scriptural position? How should I fulfill my role?

God help me. For, as I realize my obligation to God as His servant, my obligation to you as the family of God and the position that He has given me as the shepherd of the flock, and I realize my obligation to my wife and children, and I try to balance and fulfill all these obligations and their incumbent pressures—there's no way I can do it!

As Paul said, "Who is sufficient for these things?" (2 Cor. 2:16). But, with Paul, I thank God that our sufficiency is not of ourselves. Our sufficiency is of Christ. We learn to turn to Him for His help, guidance, and strength in **all** things.

Titles from Maranatha . . .

THE SOON TO BE REVEALED ANTICHRIST
By Chuck Smith. As a Christian it is always important to have the proper perspective when viewing what the Bible has to say about the Antichrist. Pastor Chuck Smith compares today's conditions with Scriptural prophecies and explains the Biblical account and timetable for the take-over by a world dictator. What's keeping the Antichrist from taking over right now?

A HANDBOOK ON CHRISTIAN DATING
By Greg Laurie. With the right attitude, dating can be a fantastic blessing for committed Christians. Pastor Greg Laurie shares the lessons he's learned from counseling with young people before and after their marriages and from his own dating experiences as a young Christian. His practical suggestions, supported by Scripture, offer encouragement and direction to singles in any age group.

SNATCHED AWAY!
By Chuck Smith. The teaching of the rapture is the greatest purifying force in the Church today. Based on an extensive study of Scripture, Pastor Chuck Smith discusses the rapture of the Church and its place on the prophetic calendar. The signs showing that the end of the world is near, and such events as the Great Tribulation and the Second Coming of Jesus Christ, are also examined in light of the Scriptures.

GOD: FELLOWSHIP OR FRUSTRATION
Randy Morich has written a spiritual guidebook for Christians that points the way to a joyous walk with the Lord. Using examples from Scripture, he illustrates God's plan for our lives. With the understanding that fellowship with God is the greatest achievement that man can attain, he explains some common causes for failure to keep the joy — and examines vital steps to the abundant life in Jesus Christ.

ATTRIBUTES OF A CHRISTIAN WOMAN
By Mike MacIntosh. A look at women in Scripture and women today. Pastor Mike MacIntosh cites that the modern woman, whether adopting or rejecting man-made and human values, isn't finding peace or joy in either case. God's way for harmony and fulfillment is explained and made real.

14736